# Latino Migrant Workers

# Hispanic Americans: Major Minority

BOTH PUERTO RICAN AND AMERICAN

CENTRAL AMERICAN IMMIGRANTS

CUBAN AMERICANS

LATINO AMERICAN CIVIL RIGHTS

LATINO AMERICAN CUISINE

LATINO AMERICANS AND IMMIGRATION LAWS

LATINO AMERICANS AND RELIGION

LATINO AMERICANS AND THEIR JOBS

LATINO ARTS IN THE UNITED STATES

LATINO FOLKLORE AND CULTURE

LATINO MIGRANT WORKERS

LATINOS TODAY

MEXICAN AMERICANS

SOUTH AMERICAN IMMIGRANTS

SPAIN ARRIVES IN THE AMERICAS

TRAILBLAZING LATINO AMERICANS

# Contents

Introduction     6

1. Who Feeds Us?     9

2. A Brief History     17

3. Fighting Back     25

4. Crossing the Border     33

5. Life on the Harvest Trail     39

6. Migrant Celebrations     47

7. What Will Happen Tomorrow?     55

Time Line     58

Find Out More     60

Picture Credits     62

Index     63

About the Author and the Consultant     64

# Introduction

by José E. Limón, Ph.D.

Even before there was a United States, Hispanics were present in what would become this country. Beginning in the sixteenth century, Spanish explorers traversed North America, and their explorations encouraged settlement as early as the sixteenth century in what is now northern New Mexico and Florida, and as late as the mid-eighteenth century in what is now southern Texas and California.

Later, in the nineteenth century, following Spain's gradual withdrawal from the New World, Mexico in particular established its own distinctive presence in what is now the southwestern part of the United States, a presence reinforced in the first half of the twentieth century by substantial immigration from that country. At the close of the nineteenth century, the U.S. war with Spain brought Cuba and Puerto Rico into an interactive relationship with the United States, the latter in a special political and economic affiliation with the United States even as American power influenced the course of almost every other Latin American country.

The books in this series remind us of these historical origins, even as each explores the present reality of different Hispanic groups. Some of these books explore the contemporary social origins—what social scientists call the "push" factors—behind the accelerating Hispanic immigration to America: political instability, economic underdevelopment and crisis, environmental degradation, impoverished or wholly absent educational systems, and other circumstances contribute to many Latin Americans deciding they will be better off in the United States.

**LATINO MIGRANT WORKERS**

And, for the most part, they will be. The vast majority come to work and work very hard, in order to earn better wages than they would back home. They fill significant labor needs in the U.S. economy and contribute to the economy through lower consumer prices and sales taxes.

When they leave their home countries, many immigrants may initially fear that they are leaving behind vital and important aspects of their home cultures: the Spanish language, kinship ties, food, music, folklore, and the arts. But as these books also make clear, culture is a fluid thing, and these native cultures are not only brought to America, they are also replenished in the United States in fascinating and novel ways. These books further suggest to us that Hispanic groups enhance American culture as a whole.

Our country—especially the young, future leaders who will read these books—can only benefit by the fair and full knowledge these authors provide about the socio-historical origins and contemporary cultural manifestations of America's Hispanic heritage.

8

# chapter 1
# WHO FEEDS US?

The United States is a country that can grow a lot of food. It has good land. And it has a lot of land. There's something growing during every month of the year. When it's snowing in the north, sunny Florida and California can still grow food. We can grow lots of different kinds of fruits and vegetables.

Every corner of the United States gives us something different. Peaches from Georgia. Blueberries from Maine. Oranges from Florida. Potatoes from Idaho. Apples from New York State. We can even grow crops in the dry Southwest. It's mostly desert out there. We just have to use fancy systems called irrigation that bring water to the plants.

All this food feeds people around the world. But there are some people who don't really get much good from all that food. Those are the people who actually grow it.

Have you ever thought about who grows your food? Sometimes it's a farmer. He or she works really hard to grow your fruits and vegetables. That's what happens on small farms. But most farms today are huge. They have hundreds and hundreds of rows of plants. Lots of people have to work on these farms. One or two farmers just can't do it by themselves.

So the people who own big farms hire workers. They hire hundreds of them. Most of the time, they hire migrant workers. These workers spend all day picking food or taking care of plants so that we can eat.

These people are called migrant workers because they don't live in one place. While they're **harvesting** food, they live in one place. Then they travel somewhere else to work on a different farm. They keep traveling all year long.

**Harvesting** *means collecting food from plants once it's ready.*

Migrant workers can be men, women, or even kids. There are lots and lots of migrant workers in the United States. The government guesses that there are almost a million people who are migrant workers. There might be even more. There could be up to three million migrant workers!

Most migrant workers weren't born in the United States. They can come from anywhere. A lot of them are from Latin America. Many migrant workers are from Mexico. Mexico is right across the southern U.S. border. Mexican people who need work can cross and find jobs. It's harder for other immigrants to come here from further away.

Sometimes migrants leave their families behind. They travel from place to place by themselves. Sometimes entire families come to the United States. They work in the fields all together.

Some migrant workers are here illegally. They're not really supposed to be in the United States. They don't have permission from the American

*Many of America's vegetables are picked by migrant workers.*

government to be here. Others are here legally. The United States government allows some people to cross the border to work on farms.

## Working Hard

So what do migrant workers do? They do a lot of different things on farms. Some plant seeds. Others help young plants grow.

When it's time to harvest the crop, a lot of migrants work at once. They pick the fruits and vegetables. They wash and dry them. They package the fruits and vegetables to be shipped to grocery stores.

Migrant farm workers work in the fields. They also work in factories where food is processed. We wouldn't be able to eat the foods we eat without migrant workers.

Farm work is hard work. Workers have to bend over to harvest fruits and vegetables. They have to carry heavy boxes filled with fruit and vegetables. And they have to spend hours and hours doing it. It's not unusual for a migrant to work twelve or fifteen hours a day.

Imagine you're picking spinach. At first, it's kind of nice to be outside. But you have to bend over to work. The sun is hot and you start to sweat. Your back is starting to hurt. You look at your watch. You've only been out here for an hour. You have eleven more hours to go. But you have to get through it.

That's how migrant workers spend each day. They aren't always given days off. They need the money for their families, so they keep working.

Even though they work so hard, migrant workers don't get paid much. The average farm worker makes $7,500 a year. Most Americans make a lot more than that. The average American makes $37,000 a year.

Some people say that foreign workers steal jobs. That's usually not

Americans depend on migrant workers' labor.

*Migrant workers go to work when the crops are ready to be harvested.*

# LATINOS AND LATIN AMERICA

There are lots of countries to the south of the United States. Most people who live in those countries speak Spanish. Some of them speak Portuguese or English. All together, all of those countries are called Latin America.

Latinos are people who come from any Latin American country. They could speak Spanish. Then we can also call them Hispanic. Or they could speak Portuguese. Or English. Or even French. Those people aren't Hispanic. But they are Latino because they live in Latin America.

true. Most Americans don't want this work. They don't want to work in a field for fifteen hours a day. They don't want to get paid so little. Farmers can't find Americans who want these jobs. So they hire migrant workers.

The farmers don't do the hiring, though. Instead, they use people called contractors. These contractors find workers. Then they hire them. Then they bring them to the grower. The contractors also pay the workers.

Most people in America have at least a little job **security**. That means that they know they'll have a job a few months from now. Migrant workers don't. Sometimes they know that they have a job for a few weeks. They can work on a farm to harvest one crop. Maybe they were hired to pick tomatoes for six weeks. They can live in a camp set up for workers for the six weeks. When six weeks are up, they

**Security** *means safety. If something is secure, you don't need to worry about losing it.*

Farmworkers face many challenges.

don't have a job. They don't have a place to live anymore either. They have to move.

Sometimes migrant workers are only hired for one day. Then they move on to find a different job. Every day, the migrant doesn't know whether he's going to work or not.

Farm workers are fired all the time. Even if they think they're working for six weeks, they might be let go sooner. When the farm work is done, the farm doesn't need workers. So it fires them. Other kinds of workers who lose their jobs can usually collect unemployment insurance from the government until they can find new work. Most migrant workers can't, though.

## Coming and Going

Where do migrant workers come from—and where do they go? A lot of migrant workers live in California, Texas, or Florida during the winter. When they're not traveling, that's where they go. Then they travel when they work. They travel from early summer through the fall. They go north to follow fruits and vegetables as they get ripe. The United States has three big streams of migrants. Lots of people move from one end to the other of those streams.

**LATINO MIGRANT WORKERS**

One "stream" goes from California to Oregon and Washington. People start in southern California. They travel north up the coast. When winter comes, they move back down south.

Another "stream" runs from Texas to Midwestern states like Ohio and Illinois. The people who follow this route work their way up the middle of the country. Some migrants go from Texas to the South. They find work in Georgia and North and South Carolina.

The third "stream" goes from Florida up the East Coast. First these workers go to the South. Then they make there way to the middle of the coast. Then they go all the way up to New England. Some travel to very northern Maine.

# Not So Different

Migrant workers may have different lives from most Americans. But they're not very different from everyone else. They all have names. They have families. They love their children, and their children love their parents.

Different migrant workers have different backgrounds. Some of them were born in the United States. Others were born in other countries.

Most migrant workers are Latino. Latino workers face a lot of challenges. They have to deal with poverty. They might leave their families

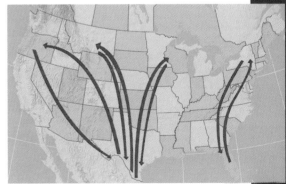

*Map of migrant workers' routes*

behind. They travel all the time. They might not speak English.

Migrant workers are important to the United States. They put food on our tables. But we don't give them much credit.

# chapter 2
# A BRIEF HISTORY

Migrant workers didn't just come from nowhere. Everyone has a history. We have to take a look at where they came from. We have to understand why they exist today.

## The Great Depression

Way back in the 1930s, something terrible happened. It was called the Great Depression.

The Great Depression was a hard time. Banks closed. People lost their jobs. Families went hungry.

Most people didn't have much money. But they needed money to buy food and clothes for their families. So they left their homes to search of work. A lot of these people went looking for farm work. There weren't that many jobs around. But people always need to eat, so there were farm jobs.

Things just got worse and worse. The weather was bad. Rain didn't fall, and crops died. It was too hot. There were big storms of dust. Insects ate

*Migrant children*

During the Great Depression, families loaded what they could into ramshackle cars and headed west, looking for work on the farms of California.

the crops that were left.

The middle of the country was so dry and dusty that people called it the Dust Bowl. There wasn't any food. Farmers couldn't make a living. So they had to leave.

It was hard to leave. Some of those families had lived on the same farm for a long time. Parents and grandparents had farmed there. That's where their friends and memories were. But they didn't have a choice. If they stayed, they might die of hunger. So they packed their bags. Where would they go?

This was the first big farm migration in America. Farm workers were traveling around, looking for work. Millions of them wanted migrant work.

Some of them went west. Their goal was California. There were big farms there. The farms hired migrant workers.

The famous author John Steinbeck wrote about the migrant workers. He wrote about the camps in California where they had to live. The camps were dirty. There was disease. People were hungry. There weren't any doctors to take care of people when they got sick.

The people who hired the migrants weren't always very nice. They didn't pay their workers much. They looked down on the migrants.

**LATINO MIGRANT WORKERS**

# Mexican Migrants

So far, we've been talking about white migrants. But there were also Mexican migrants. Where did they come from?

We have to go way back. The Mexican-American War took place during the 1840s. The United States wanted to expand. They wanted land that was owned by Mexico. One piece of land they wanted was Texas.

Texas wasn't just a huge chunk of empty land, though. Lots of people already lived there. Mexican farmers had been living there for a long time. Then, Mexico became its own country. But Texas didn't want to be part of it. It wanted to be its own country.

The United States didn't want Texas to be part of Mexico. It didn't want Texas to be its own country either. It wanted Texas to be part of the United States. So the United States took it over.

The United States wanted more land too. After the Mexican-American War, the land that is now California, Arizona, New Mexico, Colorado, Utah, and Nevada were all part of the United States.

The United States didn't just get the land, though. It also got the people who lived on the land. These were mostly Mexicans or Native Americans. Before the war they were considered Mexicans. But now they were Americans. Just like that!

Mexicans became a big part of the United States' people. More Mexicans moved up from the south. They wanted chances to get rich. There was lots of land for the taking.

*Migrant workers' housing*

Then, many years later, the Great Depression and the Dust Bowl happened. Just like the white farmers, the Mexican American farmers lost their crops too. They also had to move. Some went westward with the

**Discrimination**

*means that a group of people are treated unfairly because of the color of their skin, their religion, or something else that makes them different from others.*

**Segregated**

*means that people who are different from each other are kept separate. Schools might be segregated, for example, or public places like restaurants and restrooms.*

great stream of farm migrants. They had it even harder than the white migrants because of **discrimination**.

California was **segregated** during the 1930s. Whites could enjoy certain parks, restaurants, movie theaters, and other public places. People who weren't white couldn't go in those places. They had their own public spaces. These places were usually run down and not as good.

When Mexicans and Mexican-Americans got to California, they found segregation. They were treated worse than whites.

Some of these people were also deported. This means they were forced out of the United States and sent to Mexico. Some were American citizens. They had been born in the United States. They had never even been to Mexico before. But the United States didn't want them here.

## Things Get Bigger

Small farmers were losing their land. Small farms were disappearing, and bigger farms were growing up in their place. The people who owned the big farms got richer and more powerful.

Bigger farms meant more workers. One farmer couldn't grow crops by himself on so much land. He needed help. But he wasn't willing to pay a lot for that help.

The answer to the farmer's problem? Migrant workers. The big farm owners hired the people who had run away from the Dust Bowl. These people needed work. They were willing to work for even a small amount of money.

Farmworkers from Puerto Rico were flown to the mainland on military planes with no seating except lawn chairs.

The problems migrants had back then were the same as today. They didn't get paid well. They had long days. They worked from one day to the next, never knowing how long they would have a job.

But some people fought back. They knew they were being treated badly. Sometimes farm workers went on strike. They refused to stop working so that they would get better working conditions. Lots of strikes happened during the Great Depression.

The big farm owners didn't like the strikes. They tried to stop them. Sometimes they used violence.

## Moving Forward

Finally, the Great Depression ended. The weather got better. The Dust Bowl went away. Farmland was green again. But now a terrible war began.

The United States joined World War II in 1941. People signed up for the army. A lot of those people had been looking for farm jobs. Before there had been too many workers and not enough farm jobs. Now there weren't enough workers and and plenty of jobs.

*A **program** is an organized plan with many steps for getting something done.*

Change was in the air. Big farmers needed all the workers they could get. The United States stopped deporting Mexican Americans. The U.S. government realized that America needed Mexican Americans. They had to stay so they could work on farms.

That wasn't enough though. Farmers still needed more workers. So they decided to bring them in from Mexico.

The United States came up with a new **program**. It was called the Bracero Program. (Bracero is a Spanish word that means "a person with strong arms"). The program brought new Mexican farm workers to the United States.

**LATINO MIGRANT WORKERS**

## FIRST MEXICAN AMERICAN STATE SENATOR

Among those who worked hardest to bring an end to the Bracero Program was Henry Barbosa Gonzales. Born in Texas in 1916, Gonzales earned a bachelor's degree and a law degree before becoming the first Mexican American elected to the Texas Senate in 1961.

Not everyone was happy that more Mexicans were coming to the United States. In Los Angeles, white people started attacking any Mexican or Mexican American they could find. Even the police joined on the side of the whites.

But farmers needed the workers too much. The Bracero Program kept going. The war ended, but the program didn't. By 1960, lots and lots of bracero workers were in the United States. In fact, one out of every four people who worked on a farm was a bracero.

Braceros were treated badly. Just like during the Great Depression, farm workers didn't get paid much. They had to live in dirty camps. They worked long hours.

Things were so bad that some Americans wanted the Bracero Program to end. They wanted the workers to be treated better. The United States government ended the program in 1964.

The Bracero Program was over. But Mexican migrant work wasn't. Migrant workers kept coming. And the big farms kept paying them poorly. Pretty soon, those workers would fight back.

# chapter 3
# FIGHTING BACK

Migrant farm workers had hard lives. They traveled back and forth all the time. They didn't make much money. They worked hours and hours every day. It just wasn't fair!

One person who realized that was named César Chávez. He helped farm workers organize. Together, they fought for better working conditions.

## Who Was César Chávez?

César Chávez was born in 1927. He spent his first years on a farm in Arizona. His family had owned this farm for a while.

Chávez's grandfather was born in Mexico. Then he came to the United States. He worked in the mines in Arizona. What he really wanted to do was farm. He saved up his money and bought a farm.

The family did well. Chávez's father was in charge of the town's mail. He started three small businesses too. He opened a grocery store, a pool hall, and a garage.

The family farm was still important. All the Chávez kids grew up on the farm. César learned how to plant seeds. He learned how to pick vegetables. He learned how to take care of the animals.

Then the Great Depression came. The three businesses closed. The farm was still okay, for a while. But the Chávez's could see poverty everywhere. Migrants from the east traveled past their farm. César and his brothers and sisters went out to invite some hungry migrants in for meals.

# Becoming a Migrant

For a little while, the Chávez family kept farming. They could help others. Pretty soon, though, they needed someone to help them.

There wasn't enough rain. Their crops couldn't grow. The farm had to stop. The family went into **debt**. They had to find money to pay off that debt. César's father became a migrant. He didn't have much choice. He found work in California. So he sent for the rest of his family.

The Chávezes made it to California. But they didn't find better times there. Instead, they found sickness. They found poverty. They found sadness.

They worked and worked. They made a little money. But they didn't make enough to pay off their debt. They lost their farm. Now they didn't have a home.

The family traveled up and down the California coast. Young César went to 37 different schools. It was hard for kids like him.

People only spoke English in schools in California. They wouldn't let anyone speak Spanish. That was hard for kids who only knew Spanish. One time, César spoke Spanish in class. His teacher hung a sign around his neck that said "I am a clown, I speak Spanish."

It was hard for kids to learn like that. Lots of them dropped out of school. César dropped out of school after eighth grade. He wasn't learning. He hated school. And he had to help his family earn money.

> **Debt** *is when a person owes money. Usually, banks make loans, so people are in debt to the bank.*

*Latino farmworkers being recruited by the American government*

He started working full time in the fields. He learned a lot. He learned about farming. But he also learned about the farm workers.

He saw contractors and farm owners cheating workers. They didn't pay the workers what they were owed. He saw workers go on strike. He saw people try to work together. His father joined some farm workers groups. Once in a while, the groups won.

## Nonviolence

During World War II, Chávez joined the Navy. He was tired of working in the fields. He served two years. Then he came back. He went back to the fields.

In 1948, he married a woman named Helen. He and Helen wanted to help other people. They taught other farm workers how to read and write.

Chávez wanted to change the whole system of farm work. He wanted workers to have the rights they deserved. He started reading so he could learn how to help his people. What he read about most was nonviolent leaders. He read about Gandhi and Francis of Assisi. Both these men believed in change without violence.

So far, Chávez was just reading. He hadn't done anything yet. Then he met a man named John Ross. Ross had worked with migrants before. He knew that Latino migrants had hard lives. Ross worked with a group called the Community Service Organization (CSO). The group helped Latinos get rights. They fought discrimination. They got Latinos to vote.

## UNIONS

A union is a group of workers who get together. They fight for a common goal, like better working conditions. They might work for better pay. Or shorter workdays. Or safer places to work. Unions give workers more power. Without unions, sometimes employers can treat workers badly.

When Ross met Chávez, he convinced Chávez to start working for the CSO. Chávez started registering Latinos to vote. He realized he liked doing this sort of stuff. He wanted to help farm workers even more.

Chávez was still working in the fields. He would work long hours during the day. Then he would sign up voters in the evening. He went door to door, talking to people. He told them they could help change their lives by voting.

Chávez continued his work with the CSO. He started other CSO groups in different cities. He was even named the CSO's leader after a few years.

But he wanted to do more. He wanted big changes. He thought the best way to make things better would be to get everyone together. He wanted something big to happen.

Chávez got together with other people and thought. He talked to his wife. He also talked to a woman named Dolores Huerta. They decided to form a union. That might be a powerful way to make change without using violence.

## A Union Is Born

Chávez decided to call his union the National Farm Workers Association (NFWA). He and his group got to work.

## DOLORES HUERTA

Dolores Huerta was a teacher. She saw the struggles that migrant children faced. She said, "I couldn't stand seeing kids come to class hungry and needing shoes. I thought I could do more by organizing farm workers than by trying to teach their hungry children." She started helping migrants in the San Joaquin Valley. A lot of fruit grows there. She tried to get farm workers to sign up for Chávez's union. She made a lot of difference. She was good at going between the union and the farm owners. She helped both sides talk to each other.

They had a lot to do. Farm workers didn't have a **minimum wage.** Most workers earned between $1.00 and $1.25 an hour. $1.00 was worth more back then. But $1.00 an hour still wasn't very much money. They couldn't save money earning so little. And they could easily be fired and replaced with other workers.

To top it off, the Bracero Program started again in 1965. Farm owners didn't pay these workers much either. The Braceros had working conditions that were as bad as anyone else's. If they complained, they could be sent back to Mexico. And now there were even more workers who wanted the same number of jobs.

In 1965, some workers from the Philippines who grew grapes went on strike. The NFWA joined them. This was the group's first big strike. Everyone stopped working. They picked up signs instead.

**Minimum wage** *is the lowest dollar amount per hour that the government allows employers to pay their employees. If there is no minimum wage, than employers can pay their workers as little as they want.*

The strikers wanted raises. So they stopped working until they got the pay they wanted. The big farm owners weren't happy. They tried to use violence to get workers to go back to work.

Chávez remembered reading about nonviolence. He didn't want to respond to violence with more violence. He told everyone not to fight back. He wanted them stand up for themselves peacefully, without hurting anyone.

The season went on. The grape workers weren't picking the grapes. The fruit stayed on the vine. After a while, it rotted. The farm owners were losing money now.

The strike caught people's attention all over the country. The government sent people to look into what was going on. Chávez spoke to the government group. He told them that farm workers didn't have the same rights as everyone else. Workers in factories and offices had rights. But workers on farms didn't.

## A Strong Union

The grape-workers strike wasn't the only thing that the NSFW was doing. In 1965, it organized a march. People in California walked from San Francisco all the way to Sacramento. It was a long walk. They walked 340 miles.

The march made people pay attention. People all over the country learned about the problems that farm workers had.

*Migrant workers' housing*

The march made the farm owners pay attention, too. The owner of one of the grape farms met with the strikers. They struck a deal. The strikers got a raise and went back to work.

The NSFW merged with the Filipino group that had also been on strike. The two groups became one. It got a new name. Now it was the United Farm Workers (UFW).

Chávez and the UFW only used nonviolence. They created boycotts. This means they told people all across North America to stop buying certain foods. For example, Chávez urged people to stop eating grapes. Lots of people did. Millions and millions of people joined the movement. The farms that grew the grapes lost money if no one was buying their grapes. Pretty soon, the farm owners gave in.

*Migrant workers' sleeping quarters*

The grape boycott did even more. California governor Jerry Brown signed a new law. The law gave farm workers more rights.

Chávez even won the Martin Luther King Nonviolent Peace Award. He had done a lot to make people's lives better. And he had never used violence.

Chávez kept working. In the 1980s, he focused more on pesticides. Pesticides are poisonous chemicals that are used to kill insects on farms. They also hurt people. The farm workers that used them every day were getting sick. Chávez wanted to farmers to stop using so many pesticides.

Chávez died in 1993. Lots of people mourned his death. He had made lots of people's lives better.

His union wasn't as powerful as it used to be. There weren't as many people in it. And there are still lots of problems on big farms. But Chávez started us on a good path. People will never forget his work.

# chapter 4
# CROSSING THE BORDER

Picture the desert. There's some sand. Cactuses and bushes grow here and there. The sun glares overhead. And it's hot. Really, really hot.

It doesn't sound like somewhere you'd want to go walking. Maybe it would be fun if you were in a nice, air-conditioned car.

But thousands of people walk in the desert every year. They're not just taking a stroll, though. They're crossing the border. They're trying to find a way to get from Mexico to the United States.

## Dangerous Crossing

Many Mexicans want to get into the United States. They're looking for migrant jobs. Or they want to move to the United States permanently. There can't make any money in Mexico.

They can't just drive across the border. They're not really supposed to be in the United States. If they get caught, they'll be put in jail or sent back to Mexico. So they walk across. They walk for miles and miles in the desert. It's dangerous. People die.

As many as a million people from Latin America try to cross the United States border every year. Many people try to cross at night. The dark hides them. They're less likely to get caught. It's also cooler in the desert at night. During the day, it can reach 115 degrees Fahrenheit! At night, the temperatures aren't as hot.

The United States had put up fences along the border. They have video cameras at border crossings. Planes watch from above. People patrol the border, looking for anyone who is trying to sneak across.

All that means it's harder to cross into the United States. Lots of people cross in the middle of nowhere. There are fewer border police.

But crossing in the desert is dangerous. One person a day dies trying to get into the United States. They run out of water. Sunstroke is common. Poisonous animals live in the desert. Sometimes people get lost.

Some migrants are brought across in trucks. That's dangerous too. People are sealed up in the back of a truck. They don't have air or food. Sometimes they suffocate.

## Coyotes

The word coyote usually refers to a wild animal. But it also means people who smuggle migrants across the border.

It's hard for people to cross the border. Coyotes help them. The coyotes know the land. They know safe places on the other side. They also know how to avoid border guards.

Coyotes charge a lot of money, though. People have to pay $2,000 or more to get a coyote to help them. That's a lot of money for someone

The land along the border is often barren and rugged.

who is already poor. The whole reason they want to go to the United States is to make money. They can't make enough in Mexico.

If the border guards stop the coyote and migrants, they get sent home. The migrants don't get their money back. But people try over and over to get into the United States. Even if they get caught once, they try again. They keep raising money for coyotes.

# Conflict

Some Americans don't want Mexicans in the United States. They want them to stay home. They especially don't want illegal immigrants coming to the United States. Some of these Americans are **racist**. They don't want people who are different then them living here.

*A sign along the U.S.-Mexican border warns immigrants of extreme temperatures.*

A few people have started watching the border. They form **militia** groups. That's really a job for the police or the border guard. Or the border guards' job. But regular people want to catch illegal migrants.

Militia groups are breaking the law. But these groups scare migrants. They carry guns. They beat people up. Someday people might get killed.

> People who are **racist** think people whose skin is a different a color are not as good as they are.
>
> A **militia** is a volunteer army formed by ordinary people instead of the government.

# Why Migrate?

Migrants face a lot of challenges crossing the border. But to them, it's worth it. If they stay in Mexico, they know they can't make enough money. Most people in Mexico are poor. They don't have much hope of getting out of poverty. There isn't any work. How will their families survive?

Even the low wages they can get in the United States are better than nothing. Farm work is better than what they can find in Mexico. When a migrant makes money in the United States, he or she can send it back to their families in Mexico. They can help the people they love.

**LATINO MIGRANT WORKERS**

# Welcoming Mexicans

Some people don't want Mexicans in the United States. But lots of people think it's just fine. There are lots of Latinos here already. Many of them are from Mexico.

Mexicans add a lot to our country. They pick our vegetables. We try their recipes. Mexicans are politicians, business owners, and teachers.

Mexicans in the United States are also important to Mexico. They send lots of money back. They send billions of dollars to friends and family still in Mexico.

Unfortunately, not all Mexican migrants have good lives here. Some are successful. Others struggle. They don't get paid well, so it's hard to save up money. They live in run-down camps or apartments. They face racism and discrimination.

Migrant workers have it especially tough.

The border

# chapter 5
# LIFE ON THE HARVEST TRAIL

The migrant life is hard. It doesn't matter where migrants are based, or where they come from. Not living in one place has a lot of challenges.

## Housing

Good housing is a pretty basic need. You need a roof over your head. You need a safe place to sleep. You need enough room to live in. But many migrant workers don't even have that.

To save money, some migrants live with too many other people. Instead of spending money on housing, migrants send it to their families. So they cram in a lot of people in one apartment. Then they share rent. Ten or twelve people could live in one small trailer or apartment. A bed is a luxury in these places. People sleep on the floor. They share the floor with cockroaches and rats.

And not everyone lives in a house or apartment. People live wherever they can. That might be a cave. Or a toolshed. Or a garage. Or a parking lot.

Some farms and other work places offer housing. By law, this housing has to meet certain requirements. The government is supposed to look at the housing to make sure it's okay. But that doesn't always happen. Employers get away with providing poor housing. Or they don't provide housing at all.

# Dangerous Workplace

Potato pickers

Farm work can be dangerous. César Chávez spent a long time fighting pesticides. They're still around today, though.

Big farms use a lot of pesticides. These chemicals kill insects. They also hurt people. They hurt the people who end up eating food that has pesticides on it. They also hurt farm workers.

Farm workers spray pesticides on plants. They pick fruits and vegetables with pesticides on them. And then they get sick.

Pesticides cause skin rashes. They can make your eyes sore. They can make you feel sick to your stomach.

Pesticides can also cause more serious sickness. Farm workers are in danger if they use pesticides every day. Pesticides lead to brain damage. The liver and kidneys could get sick too. Many pesticides cause cancer.

In the past, farmers would spray their fields with chemicals while farm workers were in the field. A plane would fly over. It would dump the pesticides on the field. Below, the workers would feel the pesticides fall down like rain. They couldn't breath. Their skin burned.

That doesn't normally happen today. But workers still touch pesticides all the time. They breathe them in from other fields too.

Not all farmworkers have access to good sanitation either. Sanitation means clean toilets. It means running sinks and showers. It means good drinking water. These are all basic parts of life.

Can you imagine working for fifteen hours without a bathroom? This is how some migrants work.

Without sinks or showers, farmworkers can't wash all those pesticides off. They get even sicker. People who can wash them off are healthier.

The farm work itself is hard too. You can stand up straight to pick some things—but you have to bend over to pick strawberries, carrots, and celery. People spend all day bent over. Their backs start to hurt. After a while, their backs may be permanently damaged.

Farm workers who do get sick don't usually go to the doctor. Doctors cost too much money. And if someone is in the United States illegally, she might be afraid to go to the doctor.

Farm workers don't live as long as other people. The average American lives to be at least seventy-five. The average migrant worker will only live to be forty-nine.

*Latino immigrants plan for financial future for both themselves and their families.*

Chances are, these apples were picked by migrant workers.

*The children of migrant workers have always faced hard times that most children never experience. These children during America's Great Depression had to go with their parents across the country, living in makeshift homes like the one shown here.*

Why are farm workers' lives so much shorter? Because they get sick more often—and when they do, they usually don't have good medical care. They may have accidents. Farms are dangerous places. People get hurt on tractors. Other farm machinery can cause accidents as well.

## Kids

The kids of migrant workers have their own challenges. Some of them struggle in school. Others struggle in the fields.

Kids as young as 14 are allowed to work in the field. The law says they have to go to school too—but not all kids do. They work instead. Some kids younger than fourteen do farm work by their parents' side. Their families need the money.

Kids who are at least 16 can drive tractors and other machines. They can work with pesticides. This is only true on farms. In all other jobs, only adults can do those things.

Kids' education also suffers. If they're in the fields, they're probably not in school. They're not learning how to read and write and do math. Migrant worker children might not speak English, either. It's hard to learn in school if they don't speak English. Not all schools have programs to help them learn the language. Then there's the fact that migrants move around all the time. They follow the harvest. So do their kids. Kids

Strawberries are just one of the many crops picked by migrant workers.

move from one state to another. They start a different school every month. It's hard to learn when you have a different teacher every month. It's hard to make friends.

The children of migrant workers often don't finish school. The average kid stays in school until sixth grade. Then they drop out. Some kids don't even start school to begin with. This means that when they grow up, it will be harder for them to find another kind of job. The only kind of work they'll know how to do is farm work, just like their parents.

The homes provided for farmworkers are substandard.

# Laws

A few laws protect migrant workers. One law says that employers have to tell workers how much they're going to get paid. Then they have to actually pay them that amount.

That doesn't mean that contractors and farm owners don't break the law, though. They don't always pay workers what they should. They take the money for themselves.

Migrant workers can't fight back. Many don't know English. They don't have money. They haven't been to school. Or they're illegal. If they report the problems, they might be sent out of the United States.

The laws are getting better. But they have a long way to go.

# chapter 6
# MIGRANT CELEBRATIONS

A migrant life is a lot of work. But migrants also take time for happiness. They make art and music. They celebrate holidays. They keep their **cultures** alive. They may have left their countries, but they still hold on to their **traditions**.

One of the ways that migrant workers get through the day is their community. Community is important. Your community is the the people with whom you share things in common. You might live in the same place. You might share the same interests. You might have the same history. You might believe the same things about God. There are lots of different communities.

Think about yourself. What communities do you belong to? If you're a student, then you belong to your school's community. Maybe you like to play volleyball. Lots of your friends do too. You're part of the volleyball community.

You're also part of bigger communities. Your town is one. So is your state. And your country. Maybe your family comes from a different country. You're part of that community too. That's a lot of communities!

All those communities are good for us. They help us make friends. They help us find jobs. They help us know who we are. They help make life good.

**Cultures** *are groups' shared ways of doing things. Language, religion, food, beliefs, and customs are all part of culture.*

**Traditions** *are ways of doing things that have been handed down from grandparents to parents to children.*

Latinos in the United States belong to the Latino community. They also belong to the community of whatever country they came from. Mexicans and Mexican Americans are part of one community. Puerto Ricans are part of another.

Migrant workers have their own community. They celebrate with it. They talk about their problems. They find friends there. Their community is based on the different countries they came from. It also is a unique community all its own.

## Art

Back in the 1960s, some farm workers put together a theater group. It was called the Farmworker Theater.

This theater traveled around from place to place. It put on funny plays. But underneath the jokes, the plays were serious. They showed the problems that farm workers faced. They taught farm workers that they had rights.

> **Murals** *are very large paintings, often painted on a wall.*

Since then, Farmworker Theater has gotten bigger. It even had a Broadway show! The theater put on shows in Mexico, Central America, and Europe.

Other artists have used painting to show migrant worker problems. Carlos Almaráz is one of them. He painted **murals** that showed farm workers. Lots of people could see just what the workers had to deal with. Some artists use sculptures to do the same thing.

## Holidays

Even migrants who are far from home can celebrate holidays! There are lots of holidays to choose from.

**LATINO MIGRANT WORKERS**

*Migrant workers' rich cultural heritage adds hope to their lives.*

Mexican migrants can celebrate Mexican Independence Day on September 15. People eat a lot, dance, sing, and play sports. They celebrate all together. Kids take turn trying to burst open a piñata filled with candy. Adults swap news and take turns dancing. It's a good time to forget the troubles of everyday life.

Other celebrations are at home. Some migrant families don't get to see each other much. When they do have time together, they make the most of it.

A traditional Latino dance

One family celebration is the *quinceañera*, sometimes shortened to just *quince*. That is a party given by parents for a daughter who is turning 15. It's more than just another birthday. It marks the time when a girl starts becoming an adult. She'll have more responsibilities.

A *quince* is very exciting. Girls look forward to it years beforehand. The girl turning 15 wears a special dress. The day starts with a Catholic service. Then afterward is a dinner and a dance. A girl's whole family and all her friends are there.

It's hard when a migrant worker can't be home for a celebration. He or she is working hard to make money for his family. Sometimes families travel together. Other times only one member is in the United States. The rest are left behind.

If a migrant worker goes home to celebrate, he or she has to figure out how to cross the border again into the United States. Traveling can cost a lot of money. It's not always worth it.

# Religion

Religion is important to a lot of migrant workers. Most migrant workers are some type of Christian. When the Spanish came to Latin American a long time ago, they were Christian. They spread their religion when they took over. Now, most Latinos are also Christian.

Some religious groups help migrants. One is the Catholic Migrant Farmworker Network. It gives religious services right in the fields. That way migrants can still work, but they can also go to church.

Usually people go to church on Sunday. But a lot of migrants work on Sunday. They can't go to church. So groups that can bring religion to them are very helpful.

Religion, art, and celebrations help migrants enjoy life. These things help them hold on to their culture, even if they're moving around from place to place. They make them stronger. They keep their hope alive.

*Most Latinos are Roman Catholics.*

*Migrant workers attend church when they are able.*

# chapter 7
# WHAT WILL HAPPEN TOMORROW?

Big farms don't look like they're going away any time soon. They'll always need workers. So migrant workers will probably be around for a long time too.

But they don't have to be so poor. They can have better lives. How can we make sure that happens?

## Shopping Right

You can help!

Migrant workers pick fruits and vegetable for us. We support the migrant worker system when we buy those fruits and vegetables. César Chávez once organized a grape boycott. He convinced people to stop buying grapes from California. When people stopped buying grapes, the companies that grew them stopped making money. They had to give in to the farm workers if they wanted to keep making money.

We can do that again. We can let farms know that we don't like how they treat their workers. Do some research! Find out who works to grow the food you eat. Then write to those companies. Or stop buying their food. Tell your friends. Tell your parents and grandparents.

Shop smart. Chávez's United Farmworkers of America is still around. They have made it easier for people to choose food that was picked by workers with better lives. Look for a black eagle on certain foods. Then you know that the workers who picked or made it are treated well.

Farms will get the message if we let them know that we want them to treat workers better. Things will change!

## Latino Support

A lot of Latinos live in the United States. There are more every day. They're the fastest-growing group of people in the whole country.

Most of those Latinos live here legally. They aren't migrants. But they care about migrant workers. Maybe they know someone who is a migrant. Or a lot of someones.

Latinos can have a big say in what goes on in this country. They can vote. They can choose what to buy. They can make TV shows or advertisements.

If all Latinos worked together to help migrants, good things could happen. They can tell other people what's going on.

We should all work to make migrants' lives better. We eat the food that they pick. So we are responsible for where they work.

Learn more about farm workers' lives. Tell other people! All together we can change things for the better.

*As long as Americans grow food, they will need someone to pick it.*

# Time Line

**1840**  The United States wins the Mexican American War.

**1927**  César Chávez is born.

**1934**  The Great Depression begins. People leave their farms and travel west, looking for work.

**1941**  World War II begins. Because so many men are away at war, the United States needs workers for its farms.

**1942**  The Bracero Program begins, which allows Mexican farm workers to enter the United States.

1962  César Chávez starts the National Farm Worker Association (NFWA).

1964  The United States ends the Bracero Program.

1965  The Bracero Program starts up again.

The Farmworker Theater is formed.

The NFWA strikes against the grape growers.

1993  César Chávez dies.

2000  California creates a state holiday to honor César Chávez.

# Find Out More

## IN BOOKS

Ancona, George. *Harvest*. Tarrytown, New York: Marshall Cavendish, 2001.

Barger, W.K., and Ernesto M. Reza. *The Farm Labor Movement in the Midwest: Social Jiménez, Francisco*. La Mariposa. Boston, Mass.: Houghton Mifflin Company, 2008.

Martinez, Ruben. *Crossing Over: A Mexican Family on the Migrant Trail.* New York: St. Martin's Press, 2001.

Ryan, Pam Munoz. *Esperanza Rising*. New York: Scholastic Paperbacks, 2002.

# ON THE INTERNET

**Cornell Migrant Program**
www.farmworkers.cornell.edu

**Farmworker Justice Fund Inc.**
www.fwjustice.org

**The Farmworkers Website**
www.farmworkers.org

**Geneseo Migrant Center**
www.migrant.net

**Migration Dialogue**
www.migration.ucdavis.edu

# Picture Credits

# Index

Almaráz, Carlos 48

border 5, 10, 33–37, 52
boycotts 31, 55
Bracero Program 22, 23, 29

Chávez, César 25, 31, 40, 55
Christian 52
Community Service Organiza
    tion (CSO) 27, 28
contractors 13, 27, 45
coyote 34
culture 47, 52

discrimination 20, 27, 37
Dust Bowl 18–20, 22

Farmworkers Theater 48

Gonzales, Henry Barbosa 23
Great Depression 17–19, 22, 23, 25

harvesting 10

Huerta, Dolores 28, 29

Martin Luther King Nonviolent
    Peace Award 31
militia 36

National Farm Workers Asso
    ciation (NFWA) 28, 29
Navy 27

pesticides 31, 40, 41, 44

quinceañera 51

Ross, John 27, 28

segregated 20

union 28–31
United Farm Workers (UFW) 31

World War II 22, 27

# About the Author and the Consultant

Frank DePietro is an editor and author who lives in Upstate New York. He studied anthropology in college, and he continues to be fascinated with the world's cultures, art, and folklore.

Dr. José E. Limón is professor of Mexican-American Studies at the University of Texas at Austin where he has taught for twenty-five years. He has authored over forty articles and three books on Latino cultural studies and history. He lectures widely to academic audiences, civic groups, and K–12 educators.